MW00616765

Fly Like an Eagle

Fly Like An Eagle

101 Inspirational Poems By

David Macy

Macy International Blue Ridge, Ga.

Printed in the United States of America

Published 1998 by Macy International,
Blue Ridge, Georgia

First printing June 1998
Second Printing June 1999

Contents

Contents

Contents

Contents

Fly Like An Eagle

1 Love

A Lovely Day

It's always a lovely day,
When you give love away,
The lovely priceless treasure,
Which no one can measure.

You will be blessed by giving,
The true joy of living,
So please give it when you can,
To bless your fellow man.

Each day will be like singing,
Sweet harmony bringing,
As you give your love with grace,
In each and every place.

Everything But Love

Many folks have the finest,
All that money can buy,
But they are so lonely,
You often see them cry.

Yes in the grandest mansion,
With rich things everywhere,
It's like a barren desert,
If there's no love to share.

So these dear folks keep searching,
They search both high and low,
Because until they find love,
Their hearts will hurt them so.

O they may not realize,
This is their greatest need,
But deep within their own souls,
Something for love does plead.

A Lovely Time

It's such a lovely time,
When our sweet love we share,
Thinking of each other,
We're like the angels fair.

It's such a lovely time,
When together we pray,
Invoking God's power,
To help us day by day.

It's such a lovely time,
The world cannot imbibe,
A time of renewal,
Just shared by God's own tribe.

It's such a lovely time,
When we join hand in hand,
Our spirits entwining,
Like those in heaven's land.

Always Be Loving

Life is a sojourn,
From birth unto death,
Always be loving,
While God gives you breath.

Spread some bright sunshine,
Each step of the way,
Shining for Jesus,
By good things you say.

Live to help others,
And never to hurt,
Lifting the fallen,
From mire and the dirt.

Love is the answer,
Your fellow man needs,
By always loving,
You sow precious seeds.

People Need People

People need people,
And the love that they can give,
People need people,
There's no other way to live.

People need people,
Yes, God made us all this way,
People need people,
And we need them every day.

People need people,
So much more than they need things,
People need people,
Nothing else happiness brings.

People need people,
Whether they be young or old,
People need people,
More precious than finest gold.

True Riches

Love is what makes us rich,
Not money and things,
Love does our lives enrich,
Because from God it springs.

Things are fleeting treasure,
Which will soon pass away,
Still love will give pleasure,
Through the eternal day.

May the Lord help us see,
The golden glow of love,
And how rich we will be,
When we just learn to love.

True love will not tarnish,
Like old silver and gold,
Neither will it vanish,
In the sunshine or cold.

2 Faith

The Victories are Sure

Sometimes you'll wonder how,
Sometimes you'll wonder when,
But if your faith is strong,
Sure victories you'll win.

O, it may be delayed,
The time might not be now,
But God will make a way,
All earth will humbly bow.

When the victories come,
You will praise and adore,
The one who gives to you,
Sweet triumphs more and more.

Then you can pass along,
The faith that conquers all,
Helping fellow travelers,
Win victories great and small.

Reminders

Lest we forget his mighty power,
God sends the strong winds and the rain,
Sometimes the fierce storms make us cower,
After we on our own beds have lain.

If skies were always sunny and clear,
Then we would forget our great need,
For the almighty sheltering arm,
Encircling those who take heed.

We need reminders on our journey,
As we travel life's fleeting way,
Of the power from heaven's portals,
Which can sweep down any day.

So be thankful for wind and the rain,
Reminders of our God above,
Because of His almighty power,
He is able to show us His love.

Your Faith is so Precious

Your faith is so precious,
Like diamonds in a ring,
Do not be tempted to
Trade it for anything.

Precious faith will keep you,
In the bright shining way,
Enjoying God's blessings,
Each moment of the day.

When your faith has led you,
To that city of Gold,
You'll praise Him forever,
Who did His will unfold,

As your faith grows stronger,
The clearer you will see,
The greatness of being,
A child of God and free.

You Stood by Me

Lord I was discouraged,
Yes, I was in despair,
Because I'd forgotten,
That you are always there.

Lord help me remember,
You will never leave me,
O, give me eyes of faith,
So I this truth can see.

Lord you are so faithful,
For this I praise your name,
When doubts like mountains rise,
Your love is still the same.

Winter Will Soon Be Over

Soul in a winter of trouble,
Spring is not far away,
This hardship will soon be over,
There is a brighter day.

The cold often brings us sorrow,
Only the clouds we see,
Then spring bursts forth in her beauty,
Setting our sad hearts free.

Cling to your faith in the winter,
Tho rugged be the test,
Believe God will send the springtime,
Giving your soul sweet rest.

What Faith Can Do

O it amazes me,
What our faith can do,
When it does not falter,
But stays strong and true.

When we all are trusting,
In our God alone,
What we can accomplish,
Is not fully known.

Like a shining rainbow,
Appearing on high,
O the grace and beauty,
When faith brings God nigh.

No longer dependent,
On ourselves so frail,
We march on to victory,
While the faithless fail.

3 Thanksgiving

Let Us Thankful Be

Let us be thankful for every blessing,
We receive from God each day,
He is always with His love caressing,
As we walk this pilgrim way.

There are so many who are ungrateful,
For the blessings they receive,
Let us never be among their number,
Or to their example cleave.

God showers us with so many blessings,
From his throne room up above,
We should nere forget to thank and praise him,
As he pours out His great love.

I'll Be Happy Today

Today is the day I'll be happy,
Today is the day I'll believe,
Because I am loving and happy,
The very best I will receive.

I will not wait until tomorrow,
To enjoy each moment and hour,
I will live today to the fullest,
Knowing joy will give me power.

For so many things I am thankful,
I really cannot count them all,
This day will give me even more things,
Which will make me prostrate fall.

Until You Came Near

I felt like a lonely sparrow,
Hiding somewhere on high,
Until You came near to bless me,
Brought your sweet mercies nigh.

I know there are many others,
So desperate like me,
I want to tell them the answer,
Is your true child to be.

O every day now I marvel,
As you bless more and more,
With friendship and the true riches,
I have come to adore.

I Will Give Thanks Forever

I will give thanks forever,
To thee, O Lord my God,
For your love and blessings,
And for your chastening rod.

I won't be in that number,
Who never thank and praise,
Lord, I will do it gladly,
The loudest anthems raise.

O I am truly grateful,
For mercy from above,
What I could never pay for,
It's mine because of love.

4 Trust

God Takes Care of All

When angry foes assail you,
And life seems so unfair,
Always look up toward heaven,
Remember God is there.

Puny men have no power,
Except what God does give,
Always trust him to help you,
The one who lets you live.

With His strong arms around you,
His shield before your face,
Joys and sorrows will show you,
The riches of His grace.

Count It All Joy

Don't give up in despair,
When the sky is not fair,
You know there's a reason,
For this trying season.

This road will patience give,
Helping you always to live,
Trusting in God's strong hand,
When dreams shall turn to sand.

Where there's joy in trial,
How bright will be your smile,
When God sends from above,
The rewards of His love.

With darkness behind you,
And your pathway all new,
O how strong you will be,
From fear you will be free.

Remember the Babies

Since God takes care of helpless babies,
You know He will take care of you,
If you'll only trust in His power,
Then try His blessed will to do.

Tiny babies cannot help themselves,
They are dependent on others,
God provides a precious way for them,
By giving them loving mothers.

The sweet babies a lesson should be,
When our faith begins to falter,
Our God daily taking care of them,
Shows our care He will not alter.

He Takes The Fear Away

So many are afraid,
They fear both night and day,
When God is our Father,
He takes the fear away.

With his shield around us,
His love within our hearts,
Fear no more can haunt us,
How quickly it departs.

When we really trust Him,
We're folded in his arms,
There we rest so sweetly,
Nere fearing him who harms.

Only One Thing to Trust In

Fortunes are lost in a moment,
Dreams are shattered in an hour,
There's only one thing to trust in,
It's you O Lord and your power.

The strongest men often fail me,
When needs hover like a cloud,
Use a cloak of disappointment,
My sad weary heart to shroud.

O Lord I have learned my lesson,
In life's school I've learned it well,
If I trust in anything else,
It only sadness can spell.

How bright the way before me,
Now that my path is clear,
Every moment I'll be trusting,
The one who is always near.

The Flame May Be Burning

When all your hope seems gone,
The flame may be burning,
God working in secret,
Because of your yearning.

Be still and wait on Him,
Until you can see the flame,
Then you'll see His power,
Is through the years the same.

When hidden flames are seen,
The heart's joy is boundless,
And we see once again,
All our fears are foundless.

Dependent on Thee

How often we take God for granted,
And think we are earning our way,
Never thinking how dependent we are,
Every moment of each day.

As long as precious rain is falling,
And the sun is shining bright,
We tend to just forget the giver,
The giver of darkness and light.

When suddenly the rain stops falling,
Things are turning barren and brown,
We begin to think how dependent,
We are on our God of renown.

When will we learn to thank and praise Him,
In both the good times and the lean?
Realize our total dependence,
On the one who's real, but unseen.

And Still We Praise Him

O this life is fraught with,
Some dark times of testing,
But even in those times,
Our Father is blessing.

If we will only look for,
The rich gifts from above,
In the depths of trial,
We still see God's great love.

There must be some trials,
Along with the blessings,
When we accept this,
We feel God's caressing.

It is not our portion,
To understand each time,
We just learn to trust Him,
And this makes life sublime.

O this gives peace of mind,
Knowing our God is there,
In the deepest valley,
Ready our burdens to bear.

I Will Trust Thy Mercies Forever

I'll trust thy mercies forever
O Lord of heaven and earth,
Knowing thy marvelous power,
Shining angels praise thy worth.

Tho others trust in their riches,
Or even in self alone,
Lord, I will trust in the mercies,
Which all my life you have shown.

These sweet mercies will sustain me,
Through every trial and grief,
When my ship seems to be sinking,
When it is tossed on a reef.

When someday I shall reach glory,
When I know heaven as home,
Thy mercies will be overflowing,
As in thy garden I roam.

That's The Way Life Is

Gladness can turn to sadness,
In a moment of time,
Laughing can turn to crying,
Fast as a clock can chime.

If you think all is secure,
Your picture is not true,
Soon something will destroy it,
There will be troubles new.

The wise will trust in Jesus,
Whatever comes their way,
Looking for a better home,
Which He will give someday.

The thrill of earthly riches,
Soon fades like sunsets gleam,
Tho one has worked a lifetime,
Chasing his golden dream.

God Knows How It Shall Be

I sometimes worry,
Tho I know it is wrong,
Because of my weakness,
I am not always strong.

Soon I see the reason,
For present valleys dim,
Once more I'm reminded,
To only trust in him.

He who guides the future,
Each day takes care of me,
This is all that's needed,
Now this I clearly see.

Your Life Is In God's Hands

Your life is in God's hands,
Not in the hands of fate,
So trust Him every hour,
On His rich mercy wait.

Tis the key to living,
Knowing who's in control,
He will guide you safely,
To the home of the soul.

His hands will uplift you,
You'll be safe and secure,
Tho fiercest storms assail you,
Your anchor will be sure.

The Only One

He's the only one who really matters,
He's the only one who can reward,
He's the one who lives up in heaven,
He's the lovely precious caring Lord.

When your good deeds seem to go unnoticed,
When no one seems to see or care,
Look toward heaven and think of Jesus,
Like him someday a crown you will wear.

Lazarus was unnoticed by the masses,
Lived an earthly life of shame and strife,
Then he was carried by the angels,
To the land of endless life.

Trust in God, he will reward and bless you,
Because he has promised in his word,
The acclaim you'll receive in heaven,
Will be greater than anything men have heard.

The Whole Earth is Our Friend

The whole earth is our friend,
When on God we depend,
The shores will give treasures,
The rivers give blessings.

Nature will give it's all,
For our needs great and small,
Of this God will make sure,
Because our hearts are pure.

With the mountains serving,
The valleys caressing,
Our fleeting days below,
Will God's sweet goodness know.

The earth will be our friend,
When our bodies descend,
Our spirits will be free,
Heaven's beauty to see.

God Always Keeps His Word

I have learned by testing,
God always keeps his word,
He is always giving,
As swiftly as a bird.

This gives me an anchor,
Whatever life may bring,
God will soon be sending,
A gift on joyful wing.

With no doubt to hinder,
Or cloud the light of day,
I'll gladly trust Him,
His blessed will obey.

I will ever praise him,
For being good and true,
A dear loving Father,
Who vowed his will to do.

That's All I Need to Know

I do not fear tomorrow,
With it's joy or sorrow,
Because God is with me,
My helper he will be.

If I will just trust him,
In paths both bright and dim,
He will guide both word and deed,
And give me all I need.

Yes what others may do,
Whether hurtful or true,
Will fall like a shadow,
Because this truth I know.

Relying on God

When we rely on God,
We win more and more,
How great are his blessings,
From His endless store.

When needs are like mountains,
Looming in our way,
The path o'er these mountains,
Will be bright as day.

Our faith will grow stronger,
Each time God comes thru,
Confirming His promise,
To always be true.

If You Will Be Still

The Lord will give you rest,
Tho storms around you rage,
Soon all will be helpless,
Who would a battle wage.

If you will trust in Him,
Soon you will see the light,
Where once there was turmoil,
There will be peace and right.

He will give you calmness,
Tho black may be the sea,
You will hear Him calling,
"Dear child, just come to Me."

My Trust is In Thee

My trust is in thee O Lord,
Your promise of reward,
Help me not to forget this,
Be lured by earthly bliss.

I know that men will fail me,
On life's most rugged sea,
But you reach out in mercy,
To set my sad heart free.

Lord each day I learn some more,
Of what you have in store,
Because I trust in your love,
You're leading me above.

With your great wisdom guiding,
I now am confiding,
I know I will reach glory,
After life's brief story.

5 Prayer

Heaven's Phone

I can't make it here alone,
That's why I pick up heaven's phone,
I dial the throne room above,
Ask for Him who is full of love.

There's a direct line to Him,
Whose sweet love will never grow dim,
This line is the gift of prayer,
I know my Father is always there.

Anytime both day and night
I know how to make wrong things right,
I dial my God in glory,
Soon there is a different story.

I keep my phone close to me,
Beside me where it ought to be,
Now I can live without fear,
Because my Lord is always near.

Daddies Prayers

Daddies prayers still fill the air,
Whether skies be gray or fair,
Giving hope and cheer each day,
God will show me the way.

I can see his head bowed low,
Because he loved us so,
Asking God to give the best,
So we could face each test.

His voice was so deep and strong,
He just could not be wrong,
I knew when he prayed for me,
Soon good things I would see.

Daddies up in heaven now,
I'm glad he showed me how,
To pray about everything,
And the old hymn songs sing.

O Hear My Prayer

I'm asking you to bless,
Me through the pain and stress,
On life's uncertain sea,
Help me your hand to see.

When the waves surge and roll,
Send sweet peace to my soul,
Also your love renew,
A love that's good and true.

I know I'm needing thee,
Close by my side to be,
Come now and share my life,
Through all my toils and strife.

Yes, in your arms I'll rest,
Because you give the best,
E'n when you answer no,
I know you love me so.

You Can Touch the World

Fervent prayer touches the world,
When it's humbly given,
When you quietly repose,
After you have striven.

Never think it is small,
When for others you pray,
Tho oceans separate,
They seem so far away.

You may make a difference,
Between defeat and gain,
When in simple trusting faith,
Others needs you have lain.

These needs rise up to heaven,
To God's almighty throne,
With love He gladly answers,
The requests of his own.

Do Not Leave Me Father

Do not leave me Father,
I can't make it alone,
I need your help each day,
This to me you've made known.

Do not leave me Father,
When trials come like rain,
I need your great wisdom,
To turn them into gain.

Do not leave me Father,
When others run away,
Then I'll need you closer,
To change the night to day.

Do not leave me Father,
This is my greatest need,
To have you beside me,
For this one gift I plead.

God Hears From Heaven

God hears from heaven,
When we humbly pray,
He wants to bless us,
Each hour of the day.

Soon blessings fall,
Like the sparkling rain,
When in faith's warm bosom,
We trusting have lain.

Like flowers beauty,
The answers we'll see,
Because God wants us,
His goodness to see.

Until We Humbly Pray

Nothing really happens,
Until we humbly pray,
God hears his dear Children,
Soon help is on the way.

When He sees we're trusting,
Depending on His love,
Then His hand starts moving,
To help us from above.

In spite of our failures,
And what has gone before,
When He sees us praying,
He draws from heaven's store.

Yes, this is the secret,
When needs like mountains rise,
Pray to God believing,
The answer's in the skies.

Teach Me to Pray

Teach me to pray O Lord,
Yes teach me today,
So I can talk with you,
Each step of the way.

I know prayer is the key,
To all that I need,
So I long to know more,
About how I should plead.

I know there is power,
In prevailing prayer,
You will gladly draw near,
Give me gifts so fair.

After You have taught me,
The joy will be mine,
Each time I come seeking,
Your blessings divine.

6 Service

They Can a Blessing Be

Even our darkest trials,
Can a blessing be,
If a servant to others,
They help us to be.

They teach us how to comfort,
Hearts bowed down with grief,
Lead them gently to Jesus,
Who brings sweet relief.

Deep hurts bring compassion,
We have never known,
To many who are suffering,
This is freely shown.

Then we see God's wisdom,
In our darkest hour,
He is molding and shaping,
Giving us new power.

Things Are Not the Answer

When I see happy faces,
On those who are so poor,
It just proves the Bible,
Is a stream of truth so pure.

God's word tells us quite plainly,
We read it in His will,
Only helping others,
Will our deepest needs fulfill.

All of our earthly strivings,
To gain the things of clay,
Do not give peace of mind,
Or take our burdens away.

True service is the answer,
It gives us inward joy,
As we follow Jesus,
Give ourselves to God's employ.

Life is So Fragile

Life is like a fragile piece of glass,
That can be broken by a touch,
That's why we should do the best we can,
Together we can do so much.

We can't afford to just do nothing,
Since fragile life our portion is,
We should spend time the good pursuing,
Because the Lord has made us His.

It is God's will that life is fragile,
So fleeting are the hands of time,
If we use life to bring Him glory,
We shall hear heaven's chime.

We are here to love one another,
By doing good deeds every day,
If we do this always rejoicing,
We will just fly away.

Another Sunrise

O, Father you have blessed me,
With another shining day,
Help me to be a blessing,
To someone along the way.

I know what is important,
What will last eternally,
It is my humble service,
That I like your Son might be.

Each sunrise has it's beauty,
A gift only you can give,
It is our morning blessing,
So we can joyfully live.

You Touch Your Own

When you touch the lives of others,
You always touch your own,
From your deeds of love and kindness,
You reap what you have sown.

When you touch the lives of others,
It's a wonderful thing,
Yes, sparkling rivers of blessing,
From this sweet fountain spring.

When you touch the lives of others,
God answers your prayers,
Even when this life is cruel,
He soon the hurt repairs.

When you touch the lives of others,
Joy with you will abide,
Jesus will always be near you,
In His love you can hide.

A Slender Thread

Life is suspended by a thread,
Which can break at any time,
This is why we should Christlike be,
Keep our lives pure and sublime.

We should all do some good each day,
Pray and keep our Bibles read,
Because this life is so fragile,
Held up by a single thread.

We must keep our candles burning,
Never let our lights grow dim,
Because life may soon be ending,
Always try to live like Him.

Love your brother and your neighbor,
Show this love along the way,
Make each hour a precious treasure,
Life is just a fleeting day.

We Shall Carry Nothing Away

No matter what we store,
In havens on this earth,
We all will be leaving here,
With what we had at birth.

Many would like to take,
Treasures up in the sky,
But they'll be left behind,
The day that we shall die.

So why make this our goal,
To lay up treasures here,
Knowing our time is short,
Departure day is near.

What we send on ahead,
By doing good each day,
Will bless us forever,
Beyond the milky way.

One Drop of Rain

One drop of rain follows another,
This is the way blessings follow love,
Kind deeds are never unrewarded,
They're rewarded by our God above.

One drop of rain follows another,
Giving cheer to the dry thirsty earth,
By our kind deeds we bring happiness,
And replace gloomy darkness with mirth.

One drop of rain follows another,
Floating like pure diamonds from the sky,
When we are spreading our love and cheer,
We're a blessing like rain from on high.

One drop of rain follows another,
And sometimes the sun is still shining,
Reminding us we can sunlight be,
Yes, we can be the silver lining.

When We Warm the Hands of Others

Any act of love and kindness,
We never do alone,
When we warm the hands of others,
We always warm our own.

When we give these acts of kindness,
They come from God above,
Showing others we're his children,
Who daily live to love.

Yes, we really need each other,
As through this life we go,
We can really be a blessing,
While we live here below.

When we warm the hands of others,
We warm their hearts up too,
And they will never forget us,
Or love that's really true.

Let a Light Shine

Let a light shine from my heart,
A light to richly bless others,
Showing them there is a way,
We can be sisters and brothers.

May my light a lighthouse be,
A shining beacon in the night,
Guiding others to Jesus,
The purest everlasting light.

Let me shine each passing hour,
In this old dark and sinful world,
Let my light so radiant be,
The precious truth will be unfurled.

It is so thrilling to know,
My light can shine where e're I go,
Shine for my blessed Jesus,
The one who loved me so.

Help Me a Lovelight to Be

Help me, O Lord, a lovelight to be,
That many might our Savior see,
Help me to shine brightly each day,
That many might walk heaven's way.

Help me to shine in sorrow and pain,
Knowing I have glory to gain,
Then all these swift troubles and trials,
Will fade into heaven's smiles.

Let the love you have placed in my soul,
From my lips like sweet anthems roll,
Telling those who are lost in their sin,
How they can a victory win.

Help me reflect your love and your grace,
When others look upon my face,
May it shine with a lovelight so pure,
They'll know the way that is sure.

Tomorrow May be Too Late

Do the good you are planning today,
Because tomorrow may be too late,
If you plan to show someone the way,
Please, my precious brother, do not wait.

There is a visit you need to make,
Because tomorrow may be too late,
Make the visit now, for Jesus sake,
Please, my precious sister, do not wait.

Do you need to give comfort and cheer,
Because tomorrow may be too late,
To those aching hearts your must draw near,
Please, my precious pilgrim, do not wait.

Can you give an encouraging word?
Because tomorrow may be too late,
Give it now, like a beautiful bird,
Please, my precious traveler, do not wait.

A Life Like Shadows

Tho a life like shadows comes,
And leaves like an evening breeze,
It can touch countless lives,
If lived the Lord to please.

Often days few in number,
Burn like a candle bright,
Showing many the Savior,
Bathed in beauty and light.

The days that we are pilgrims,
Does not the story tell,
It's how we spend our moments,
In sin or serving well.

Often a life like shadows,
Does more to bless the land,
Than many who live longer,
But never hold God's hand.

I Don't Know How Long

I don't know how long I'll be here,
So I will just do the best I can,
Spend my few days humbly serving,
Serving my precious fellow man.

I don't know how long I'll be here,
Like a mystery it will unfold,
I'll be busy helping others,
Until these hands lie still and cold.

I don't know how long I'll be here,
Life is filled with uncertainty,
All the days of my sojourning,
I want like my Master to be.

I don't know how long I'll be here,
In this dark land of pain and woe,
May my light always be shining,
Until to death's valley I go.

More to Life

There's more to life than having fun,
So many battles to be won,
Let's be up and doing each day,
While our lives swiftly pass away.

There's more to life than one big blast,
We need to work for things that last,
Then when earth time has come and gone,
Before our eyes will glory dawn.

There's more to life than party time,
Which all ends with morning chimes,
We need to look to future days,
By pleasing God in all our ways.

There's more to life than pleasing self,
Often we should be on the shelf,
When you really put others first,
Then pure joy from your heart will burst.

There's more to life than games of play,
Yes, so much more to do and say,
When all games are silent and still,
Will you have done God's will?

Lord, Help Me to Really Care

Lord, help me to care about people's needs,
By doing this I will sow eternal seeds,
Help me to have a loving heart like yours,
Give me a sweet compassion which endures.

Lord, help me to give, and then give some more,
By doing this I can open heaven's door,
Lord, help me to never sow sparingly,
Freely giving, I will become like thee.

Lord, open my eyes so I can see,
Let them not be looking at only me,
Help me to see all the sorrows of men,
Those who are now walking where you have been.

Help their tears and heartaches to be my own,
May they never have to suffer alone,
Help me all their heavy burdens to bear,
That your sweet name, I might worthily wear.

Set Sail for God Today

Set sail for God today,
Across life's stormy sea,
Ask him to give the wind,
You will a blessing be.

Set sail with faith within,
That all His words are true,
Asking him to use you,
His blessed will to do.

Set sail with hope anew,
That great things shall be done,
With God as your captain,
The victory shall be won.

Put Here to Serve

We are put here to serve,
Now, what about you?
For what are you living?
Is this what you do?

Do you live for pleasure,
Is this your life's goal,
Satisfying passions,
Ignoring your soul.

Please think now my brother,
And my sister too,
Spend many hours serving,
Be faithful and true.

Exceeding are the Blessings

Exceeding are the blessings,
Of those who love the Lord,
Those who will labor daily,
For heavens blest reward.

We know form God's true precepts,
We're saved by matchless grace,
But those will be rewarded,
Who will His work embrace.

O God cannot reward us,
Like those who give their all,
When divine eyes see clearly,
Our work for Him is small.

So let us rise up reapers,
Into the harvest go,
Be busy like our Master,
The one who loved us so.

7 Heaven

Set Your Heart Upon Heaven

Set not your heart on riches,
On things of earthly clay,
Set you heart upon heaven,
The bright eternal day.

Riches take wings like eagles,
Oft they're lost in a day,
But your blest home in heaven,
Will never pass away.

Be wise while here you journey,
O always look above,
Thinking of heaven's glories,
And of it's endless love.

Heaven's View

When I look at mountains,
That were made by you,
I think how alluring,
Will be heaven's view.

I know it is dazzling,
In it's glory bright,
That land of contentment,
Where there is no night.

O it's pristine beauty,
Will surpass my dreams,
Like a shining emerald,
I know that it gleams.

To think I will live there,
Yes for evermore,
Keeps me always striving,
For the prize before.

Some Day I Shall See Him

Some day I shall see Him,
In all His glory there,
The richness of His goodness,
Forever I will share.

For this day I'm living,
To see Him on his throne,
When all dark mysteries,
His wisdom shall make known.

With troubles behind me,
I will bask in His grace,
And give myself fully,
To his loving embrace.

This hope is so precious,
Nothing else can compare,
With seeing his glory,
In my homeland so fair.

The Fire is Going Out

The fire is going out in this old body,
The flame is burning lower every day,
I will soon be leaving this world of sorrow,
I'll soon be going beyond the milky way.

The fire is going out in this old body,
I know the time of my departure is near,
But I have no fear of the crossing over,
Because there my God will wipe away each tear.

The fire is going out in this old body,
This temple is crumbling more each passing day,
I know the road of life will soon be ended,
I can't wait to receive my eternal pay.

The fire is going out in this old body,
Life's embers are losing their transient glow,
The flame of joy is burning ever brighter,
Because soon to heaven's glory I shall go.

When My Captain Calls Me

When my Captain calls me,
I will be going home,
Never more to suffer,
And never more to roam.

I'm waiting for orders,
I'm listening every day,
When I hear Him calling,
I will be on my way.

With battles behind me,
I'll rest for ever more,
Where peace is eternal,
And saints have gone before.

Some Day I Will be Sailing

Some day I will be sailing,
Across the unknown sea,
Where Jesus will be waiting,
To give a mansion to me.

I do not fear the journey,
Across the straits unknown,
O angels will sail with me,
I will not be alone.

When I see walls before me,
Made of pure jasper stone,
I know I will be shouting,
"Praise God, I'm coming home."

I Know I Have a Future

All the past is behind me,
It's course I cannot change,
Some of the things that happened,
Now to me seem so strange.

I don't know how long I have,
To live down here below,
But the place I am going,
Deep in my heart I know.

What took place in former times,
Means nothing to me now,
All my sins are forgiven,
A crown will grace my brow.

How Jesus could love me enough,
His precious life to give,
Is beyond my highest thoughts,
Until with Him I live.

I Am Longing for Heaven

I am longing for heaven,
Where a crown I will wear,
With saints from all the ages,
Who will be singing there.

I want to leave earth's troubles,
All the sorrow and pain,
Be near the lovely bosom,
Where Jesus once has lain.

I believe every promise,
I know there is a place,
Where all the times of darkness,
God's sweet love will erase.

The Love of Heaven

We have never known love,
Like the love of heaven,
To all of God's children,
This love shall be given.

O what a reunion,
One that will never end,
When all of us loved ones,
Our happy voices blend.

We will shout in glory,
Be filled with ecstasy,
When God gives his sweet love,
And it's beauty we see.

We will fall before Him,
Who brought us to that place,
He gave up his life's blood,
To bring us saving grace.

I'll be Going Home

God will call someday,
He will call me home,
A few more trials,
Then no more I'll roam.

I will be ready,
When He calls for me,
Because I'm longing,
His dear face to see.

O hallelujah,
I will shout and sing,
Then fly to glory,
On an angel wing.

When I reach heaven,
Bow before His throne,
My lips will praise Him,
For sweet love I've known.

8 Jesus

Bring Me to the Saviour's Side

Bring me to the Saviour's side,
Where by grace I shall abide,
On the crest of troubles wave,
He will heal and He will save.

This is where I want to be,
Throughout vast eternity,
There I'll dwell in humble praise,
Use my voice his worth to raise.

He who died on Calvary,
My best friend will always be,
We will walk with mutual love,
Thankful to our God above.

When earth's victory is won,
I will live with God's own Son,
Now I cannot see the prize,
I shall see Him in the skies.

The Valleys Sing About Jesus

The valleys sing about Jesus,
How His goodness flows,
When they are bursting with increase,
Then His kindness shows.

Because He is so beautiful,
The valleys can sing,
All of the streams and the flowers,
Let His praises ring.

Sweet strains of heavenly music,
We will always hear,
When valleys sing about Jesus,
We know God is near.

The songs beautiful valleys sing,
Are always the best,
They lift up many weary hearts,
Putting them at rest.

There Is Hope

There is hope in Jesus,
No matter what you've done,
If you will obey him,
The righteous Holy one.

The cleansing of His blood,
Will make you white as snow,
This is a gift from God,
The one who loves you so.

After precious cleansing,
Each day you'll live anew,
Jesus will not leave you,
He is a friend so true.

Jesus is Lord

The rocks cry out in praise,
The trees their voices raise,
To glorify our King,
O let earth's anthems ring.

The rivers join the song,
He suffered cruel wrong,
Then died our souls to save,
How much our Saviour gave.

The mountains will be heard,
How awesome is their word,
Before Him who made all,
Their majesty will fall.

The oceans loudly roar,
And praise our Master more,
For the amazing love,
He brought down from above.

A Friend Indeed

When you come to blessed Jesus,
You will find a friend indeed,
A friend who will always love you,
And to all your cries give heed.

If vainly you have been searching,
For a friend who will be true,
Come and put your trust in Jesus,
He will give you hope anew.

There is never any pretense,
When Jesus becomes your friend,
Yes He will be true and faithful,
Until your brief life shall end.

With Jesus as your true helper,
Walking closely by your side,
You will never fear life's troubles,
In faith's path you will abide.

If Your Bed is in Darkness

If your bed is in darkness,
Jesus will give you light,
He will change all your pathways,
Making them clean and bright.

If you are tired of running,
Come to Jesus today,
He will remove the darkness,
Take all of your guilt away.

Gone will be the slavery,
Chained to a bed of woe,
Blessed freedom in Jesus,
You will forever know.

How Could He Die There

I can't understand it,
Even though I try,
How could God's beloved,
On Calvary die.

I know that He loves me,
His own life He gave,
Such love is beyond me,
Like a distant wave.

In mansions of glory,
I will understand,
But here I just marvel,
O'er God's gracious hand.

Jesus, You are Lovely

Jesus you are lovely,
Lovely in all your ways,
I will always love you,
And gladly give you praise.

What a rich blessing,
To see your loveliness,
May some of your beauty,
My humble life caress.

I believe in mercy,
In God's wonderful grace,
That it will transform me,
As I look on your face.

Radiant with your beauty,
I'll shine until I die,
Then I'll shine forever,
Praising you on high.

It's a Beautiful Thing

There's beauty in believing,
There's beauty in true love,
They're both a gift from heaven,
From the portals above.

This beauty is not purchased,
With coins made here below,
It's only found in Jesus,
When we the Saviour know.

This beauty keeps on shining,
With a radiance so bright,
When we live by God's precepts,
Walk in the blessed light.

You Will Win

If the Lord is with you,
There is nothing to fear,
Saint, keep him beside you,
Make sure that He is near.

No matter the number,
Who have become your foes,
If the Lord is with you,
They will soon come to woes.

When you win the battle,
Your foes are at your feet,
Your union with Jesus,
Will forever be sweet.

Wonderful in Jesus

It's wonderful in Jesus,
I'll sing a gladsome song,
I'm free from Satan's bondage,
I'll praise him all day long.

I still have earthly troubles,
I walk not paths of ease,
But now I live rejoicing,
Trying my Lord to please.

My eyes are now on heaven,
That bright and shining shore,
Where I shall see my Saviour,
And praise him more and more.

When We Cast Our Crowns Before Him

When we cast our crowns before him,
Then Jesus will reward,
If with all our hearts we've served him,
And worshipped Him as Lord.

We will cast our crowns with reverence,
At Jesus blessed feet,
As He sits in all his glory,
On heaven's judgment seat.

Then our waiting will be breathless,
Our longing will be true,
As we strain to hear dear Jesus,
Call us to life anew.

At last we'll see his radiance,
Shining like noonday sun,
And know throughout endless days,
Thru Him the victory's won.

I Will Ask Jesus

When I have a need,
I know where to turn,
To precious Jesus,
O He will not spurn.

I know He loves me,
He died for my sins,
Shedding His life's blood,
My pardon to win.

When I pray humbly,
I know what He will do,
Soon He will answer,
He will see me thru.

People are searching,
For so many things,
Ignoring Jesus,
And the joy He brings.

The search is ended,
When we rest in him,
No longer walking,
In sin's valleys dim.

Parents and Jesus

We are all like our parents,
In so many ways,
O let us be like Jesus,
All life's fleeting days.

We imitate our parents,
In action and speech,
We must imitate Jesus,
To blest heaven reach.

Our parents were our models,
In our days of youth,
Jesus should be our model,
In both love and truth.

We're thankful for our parents,
For the good they taught,
We are thankful for Jesus,
He salvation brought.

Yes, parents are precious,
And so is our Lord,
Thank God for good parents,
Thank God for our Lord.

9 God's Love

Beautiful Love

Beautiful cascading streams,
Remind me how God's love beams,
From his shining throne on high,
Blessing till the day I die.

Thank God for beautiful love,
Cascading down from above,
Refreshing my weary soul,
When this earth life takes its toll.

Now I feel so clean and pure,
My life is anchored and sure,
Because of beautiful love,
I am like a snow white dove.

Love led me to do His will,
Learn to trust and then be still,
I will praise Him forever,
In both word and endeavor.

Life is Like a Rose

When God's love is abiding,
Life is like a rose,
The very best life can bring,
Your daily walk knows.

This is the key to living,
Enjoying the best,
Make sure God's love is with you,
He will do the rest.

You will walk in bright sunshine,
Bathe in the purest light,
As God's sweet love flows through you,
Making your pathway bright.

You will find countless blessings,
Wherever you go,
As you live to help others,
This great love to know.

Crying for Your Love

I cry out for you O Father,
I cry out for your love,
O please send it now Jehovah,
From your shining courts above.

Lord I am not asking gently,
With smooth words I have learned,
My cry comes from deep within me,
Where so oft I have yearned.

O this is the gift more precious,
Than all the world can give,
So now I am crying Father,
For love each day I live.

Love is the Reason

When life's blessings begin to flow,
Before God's throne we should go,
Thanking Him for wonderful love,
Coming from heaven above.

Love is what opens windows wide,
Where we know God does abide,
From these windows the blessings pour,
So many there is no store.

God's heart is bigger than oceans,
Worthy of our devotions,
Daily He richly blesses all,
Who in obedience do fall.

His Song Shall be With Me

His song shall be with me,
His song of love and joy,
If I will faithful be,
Steadfast in His employ.

With His song deep within,
I can face anything,
In darkness or trial,
Peace from this song shall spring.

This is another proof,
Of His abiding love,
Blest song of cheer and hope,
From shining realms above.

You Need Him Now

You need the Lord now,
Not some other day,
He is the answer,
And salvation's way.

You need his love,
His unfailing care,
His deliverance,
From the tempter's snare.

You need the cleansing,
His shed blood can give,
Then for the first time,
You will really live.

He Drew Me Out of the Waters

He drew me out of the waters,
The dark waters of sin,
So I could His loving kindness,
Joyfully enter in.

It seemed that my life was hopeless,
I was filled with despair,
Then He lifted me to safety,
Now faith's garment I wear.

What a difference His love made,
Since I am free and clean,
Yes I am soaring to new heights,
To glories now unseen.

Still Waters

Many are away from the still waters of life,
Spending their days in sin and strife,
Until they to the precious still waters draw near,
They'll live in misery and fear.

Oh, what a joy near the deep still waters to be,
Where there's peace and tranquillity,
Knowing the almighty presence of God is there,
Helping all our burdens to bear.

Clear still waters are a touch of heaven on earth,
How much these still waters are worth,
Giving satisfaction in the depths of the soul,
Troubles o'er us just seem to roll.

These still waters drawn from wells of God's love,
Flowing down from bright heaven above,
This is the reason they are so precious and sweet,
And all of our longings they meet.

A Gift of God's Love

God gives us our families,
To bless us all our days,
Another proof of the love,
He shows in countless ways.

When we look in children's eyes,
And see the joyful light,
We should bow in thankfulness,
For love which makes things right.

When we can feel the power,
Of our families touch,
We know who gives the power,
One who loves us so much.

We will know them in heaven,
We will know them by name,
We'll be thankful forever,
From God our families came.

Nature's Chorus

Let the fields rejoice,
That God is in heaven,
Let the trees sing out,
Salvation was given.

God has given all,
This is why they praise,
They join together,
To tell His wondrous ways.

Now let the sea roar,
And all it's fullness give,
God sends down blessings,
So we can joyful live.

Let the mountains shout,
Our God they do adore,
Their words will echo,
On every earthly shore.

God Does All Things Well

God does all things well,
Whatever it might be,
This we see each day,
When from sin we're set free.

When we do His will,
Are striving to obey,
We rejoice to see,
His shining perfect way.

There is always love,
When God a task performs,
O how sweet it is,
When one his life conforms.

Goodness Will Pursue Me

Goodness will pursue me,
All the days that I live,
Knowing it will find me,
Does sweet assurance give.

Goodness will pursue me,
If I'll trust and be still,
It always finds those,
Who do the Father's will.

Goodness will pursue me,
Wherever I may go,
The steps of His children,
The Father's heart does know.

Goodness will pursue me,
In valleys deep and dark,
From their gloom and sadness,
By grace I shall embark.

My Father is Wonderful

My Father is wonderful,
My Father above,
Everyday I marvel,
At His matchless love.

Sometimes I am really weak,
My faith is not strong,
But still He is wonderful,
Righting all that's wrong.

What a joy to rest in Him,
Knowing that He cares,
With a Father's loving heart,
He my hardship shares.

Like sunshine in the morning,
His love is to me,
Each day my heartfelt desire,
Is His child to be.

God's Love is so Amazing

God's love is so amazing,
Given to us so free,
Love to bear us to heaven,
Where God's glory we'll see.

Deeper than deepest caverns,
Is the depth of his love,
Soon after darkest pathways,
It lift's us up above.

How His love does inspire us,
To love our fellow men,
Spend all of our lives striving,
To bring them out of sin.

O the joy when in glory,
Unveiled love we shall see,
Knowing our God has given,
Eternal victory.

God Never Forgets

God never forgets His children,
In their lowly estate,
In these dark times He draws nearer,
Being touched by their fate.

He knows that His children need Him,
Most when others forsake,
So He remembers and blesses,
All for His children's sake.

O never think you are friendless,
Or God has left you alone,
He is a God who remembers,
This so often He's shown.

Fly Like An Eagle

I will soar in the morning,
Above the world and it's strife,
God's pure love will surround me,
All the blest days of my life.

I have found the secret,
Of living above dark fear,
It is being in God's love,
Knowing He is always near.

O, the scenes that will bless me,
As I fly toward heaven's land,
The world will never see them,
Their joys will crumble to sand.

I will fly like an eagle,
Fly higher than a dove,
I will fly up to glory,
On the wings of God's love.

About the Author

David Macy was born in poverty in
Huntsville, Alabama. From this humble
beginning, by the grace of God, he has
had the opportunity to evangelize in
eight countries. "Fly Like An Eagle"
is David's second book. He loves both
writing and speaking. He is also a regionally
known painter in oils. David resides in
Blue Ridge, Georgia with his wife Maureen,
and their union has been blessed with seven
children.